For those who want to tell their story—may you find a way to share it with the world.

R.M.

Dedicated to the people and heroes in this book who have helped me get through my challenges and hard times.

H.M.

To those who want to leave their mark on the world. For my dad who showed me how to follow my dreams and to my family for believing it was possible.

B.D.

# REPRESENT!

30 true stories of trailblazers, artists, athletes, and
adventurers with disabilities

VOLUME ONE

Written by **ROSALIE & HUNTER MASTALER**

Illustrated by **BRANT DAY**

# A NOTE TO THE READER

## DEAR READER,

In 2015 Hunter became a below-knee amputee, and in 2017 he was diagnosed with bilateral hearing loss.

As parents, we grieved over the amputation of our child's leg and loss of hearing and wondered what to expect. We were thrown into the uncharted waters of disabilities and felt lost. What would his future be like? Over time, we watched, listened, and learned from others on a similar path as Hunter. We turned to the internet and sought out communities, finding comfort as we saw others leading happy lives while living with a disability. The more involved we became in the community, the more we noticed the lack of disability representation. Why weren't they more visible? Why weren't their stories being told? How had we not learned about these people before? All these questions led to the idea of *Represent! Vol. 1*.

It started when Hunter was eleven years old. We spent months deliberating over the people and stories we wanted in the book. At first our list of people was not very long, but the more we researched, the more stories we wanted to share. We couldn't help but add more and more! Once we decided on thirty people, we began studying and writing. We watched documentaries and videos; we scoured the internet for articles and blogs, and read story after story. We discovered so many people while working on *Represent! Vol. 1* that we might have already started a list for Volume 2. Stay tuned!

It has been a joy to study alongside Hunter. We often talk about the people in this book. A large handful of them are his heroes and have become our household names. He looks up to and admires them; he lets them lead the way as he takes on life.

We hope that as you read each story, you are inspired to continue to learn. These stories matter. The trailblazers, artists, athletes, and adventurers in this book deserve to be talked about and shared. Let them become your household names. Let them become people you look up to. Make *Represent!* more than just another book full of biographies. Let it inspire change and growth.

**Sincerely, Rosalie**

## FROM HUNTER

I love learning about people who face challenges and go after their goals and dreams. They motivate me to achieve more and do hard things.

When I became an amputee, I didn't know what I was capable of, but then I learned about people just like the ones in this book. It helped me to know that I could break through barriers I was facing and live a happy life. I know that if Erik Weihenmayer can climb the tallest mountain in the world, if Mike Coots can still love sharks, and if Cece Bell is brave enough to share her story, I can find ways to adapt, take on challenges, and persevere. When you finish this book, I hope you will keep on learning about these people and the disability community. Each person has taught me something for the better, and I am grateful to have learned about them.

**Your friend, Hunter**

# JORDAN THOMAS FOUNDATION INFO

A portion of the proceeds from Represent! Vol. 1 will be donated to the Jordan Thomas Foundation. Thank you for your support and contribution!

Jordan Thomas Foundation Mission: The Jordan Thomas Foundation returns children and adolescents to a life without physical limitation by providing quality prostheses until adulthood, serving as a caring resource for the child and family living with limb differences and tirelessly advocating for insurance fairness.

About Jordan: In 2005, Jordan was involved in a boating accident which resulted in the amputation of both legs below the knee. At only 16 years old, Jordan knew that his mission in life was to help kids in need of quality prostheses. Jordan has committed to inspiring kids to PRESS ON and live their dreams!

jordanthomasfoundation.org

# TABLE OF CONTENTS

# ERIK WEIHENMAYER

*Success is not just the crowning moment, the spiking of the ball in the end zone, or the raising of the flag on the summit. It is the whole process of reaching for a goal, and sometimes, it begins with failure.*

Erik Weihenmayer lives for adventure. From hiking the seven highest peaks in the world, to climbing into an active volcano, and kayaking down the Colorado River, Erik explores in a way people never thought possible—without sight.

Due to a rare retinal disease, Erik went blind at age thirteen. Initially, it was a challenge for him to accept his disability. Yet as he grew older, he realized that he'd lost his vision but not the ability to see and experience the world in his own way.

With a loving family and community by his side, Erik refused to sit on the sidelines. He participated in sports, wrestled for his high school team, and later became a coach. He also took up rock climbing and developed a deep love for the wilderness. He gained a sense of independence from being able to scale the side of a mountain, feeling for cracks, pockets, and grooves in the rocks. As his body adapted, his sensitivity for sound intensified—he was able to feel vibrations moving through the air and, in a way, could literally feel the space around him.

Erik's adventurous spirit has taken him around the world, but one journey that really tested his courage was kayaking the harrowing waters of the Colorado River. You have to be an experienced and daring kayaker to brave those raging rapids. And can you imagine kayaking without being able to see? But Erik did it! He journeyed down the entire 277 miles of the Grand Canyon.

In 2001 Erik became the first blind person to summit Mt. Everest, which opened the door to changing people's perception of the blind/low vision community—a community that has a wide spectrum and needs for accessibility.

Erik is most famously known for reaching the highest peak in the world, but there's more to him than his claim to fame. In 2005 Erik co-founded *No Barriers USA*—an organization whose mission is to provide experiences for those who want to break through barriers in their life. The *No Barriers* motto is a powerful reminder that Erik hopes everyone can remember:

## "What's within you is stronger than what's in your way."

Erik strives and pledges to live a "No Barriers" life and hopes to give the world the courage to explore in ways we never thought possible.

# JESSICA COX

**BORN 1983** — It's only human to have low moments in life, because if you don't, then you won't feel the high, exciting times.

Becoming a pilot is no easy feat. But, imagine flying a plane with ONLY your feet!

Jessica Cox was born without arms and was told her dream of becoming a pilot would be impossible. But Jessica believed in doing the impossible—arms or not.

Growing up, life wasn't easy for Jessica. She had to learn how to tolerate name calling and not fitting into the norm of society. She had to approach everyday tasks differently than everyone else, managing life by only using her feet. When she was a teenager, she attempted to use prosthetic arms but the bulkiness of them and the way they functioned were more of a hindrance than a help. When she gained enough confidence to go armless, she discovered a newfound freedom. Still, things like eating, getting dressed, and doing chores were all challenges she had to figure out how to do in her own way. It was a lot of trial and error, but she kept trying and adapting, and didn't give up.

In 2008, after three years of flight training, Jessica took off on her first solo flight in Arizona, USA. Wearing a shirt that said "Look Ma, no hands," she qualified to fly a light-sport airplane to altitudes of 10,000 feet. That one courageous act made aviation history and earned her a Guinness world record. But she didn't stop there. She visited and flew over Greece, the Philippines, and Ethiopia. Everywhere she went, she shared her triumph of achieving the impossible.

Jessica travels the world addressing inequalities between the disabled and non-disabled. She is working hard to fight for their rights—awareness, inclusion in schools, and equal opportunities. She lobbied for the International Disability Treaty in the USA and continues to advocate and be a mouthpiece for the disabled community.

Along with being an advocate, she champions for female pilots and champions them as they pursue their dreams in aviation.

Jessica is also a trailblazer as a martial artist! She is the first armless person to earn a black belt in American Tae Kwon Do. Believe it or not, she uses nun-chucks with her feet.

With all that Jessica has accomplished, she has shown the world that the impossible can indeed become the possible.

 # JAMES CASTLE

BORN
**1899**

DIED
**1977**

Back in 1899, James Castle was born in Idaho, USA.

Being deaf, James' days and nights were silent, but he took in the world through sight and recreated everything he saw. With only a pencil, soot from candles, or cardboard and string, he created unique art of animals, people, and household furniture. He also used envelopes his dad was the town's postmaster and worked out of their living room.

Some of James' most famous drawings were created with a sharpened stick dipped into soot scraped from a wood stove, mixed with his saliva, and turned into a paste.

James spent a lot of time in the attic, their unused ice house, and the chicken coop. For part of his life, he only had a mattress on the floor. He would often draw images of furniture and windows and hang them on the wall to create a fictional bedroom.

Growing up, James attended a school for the Deaf, but learning was a struggle for him and back then, teachers weren't given enough resources to help students who had challenges like James.

James never learned how to read or communicate with sign language. This isolated him from children in the community and they would often call him "Dummy" or "Crazy Jimmy." James' dad also struggled to connect with him and would sometimes separate James from the family.

James didn't have very much human connection, and turned to art as a lifelong companion. He cherished his creations and would keep them in boxes he constructed out of scraps. But, no matter how hard he tried to protect his art, neighborhood kids would sometimes raid his studio and destroy everything.

When James was an adult, his nephew took James' art and showed it to one of his professors. The professor was pleasantly surprised and asked to see James right away. They traveled from Portland, Oregon, to Boise, Idaho. When they arrived, the professor fell in love with James' art, took some samples and immediately organized an exhibit at the school. It was a success, and James started to make a name for himself. He eventually made enough money to buy a small house. Finally, he had something to call his own.

James may not have been able to communicate with words, but his art is a living history of his life and a legacy of his brilliant and creative mind. He will always be known as one of the greatest American artists of the twentieth century.

# ALI STROKER

**BORN 1987**

One night, in a backyard production of *Annie*, a little girl named Ali Stroker played the leading role. That was the moment when Ali felt her life begin. A spark was ignited, and the flame for musical theater started to burn.

At two years old, Ali was in a car accident that paralyzed her from the waist down, and growing up, she couldn't help but wonder if her wheelchair would make her an outcast. But theater and music gave her a place to call home.

As she grew older, she dreamed of being on Broadway, but there was no one on stage who looked like her. Still, she told herself over and over...

## "Turn your limitations into opportunities."

She stood by her motto and became the first wheelchair user to graduate from New York University's Tisch School of the Arts drama program. In 2015 she made history with her Broadway debut in *Spring Awakening* as the first wheelchair user on a Broadway stage. And then in 2019, in true trailblazer fashion, she broke down a huge barrier and became the first wheelchair user to WIN a Tony award. She won for her role as Ado Annie in *Oklahoma*, as she transformed the character into her own unique style and wowed audiences over and over again.

At the awards ceremony Ali gripped the Tony and held it high above her head. With a beaming smile she said, "This award is for every kid who is watching tonight who has a disability, who has a limitation or a challenge, who has been waiting to see themselves represented in this arena—you are."

Beyond music and theater, Ali has a knack for writing. She co-wrote a middle grade novel featuring a main character who uses a wheelchair titled, *The Chance to Fly*. One book led to another, and she now has a picture book—*Ali and the Sea Stars*. And surely she has more stories to tell.

From a backyard production all the way to the Broadway stage, Ali is now able to use her voice, not only as a singer but also as a spokesperson for the disability community. She wants everyone to have a chance to find their home in a theater. Ali advocates for theater owners to make their backstage more accessible and for musical artists with disabilities to find the courage to take to the stage.

# CHRIS NIKIC

BORN
**1999**

Not everyone dreams of completing a triathlon, but Chris Nikic was not your average dreamer. He wanted to take on the challenge but knew it was not going to be easy.

Chris has Down Syndrome—an extra chromosome which causes specific facial features, weak muscle tone (hypotonia) in infancy, and cognitive delays. Almost half are born with heart defects as well as issues with hearing and vision.

Chris had open heart surgery when he was a baby, didn't walk until he was almost four years old, and couldn't eat solid foods until he was six, which caused further physical delays.

Despite all of Chris' challenges, he still dreamed of taking his first step over the finish line and becoming an Ironman—someone who completes a grueling 140.6 miles in 17 hours by swimming, running, and biking. Chris believed in becoming 1% better every day and started working toward his goal of becoming an Ironman.

Chris' dad reached out to coaches to train Chris, but they weren't sure he was strong enough to handle the training, and they all turned him down. Even doctors were pessimistic, but Chris would say to them, "Don't tell me I'll fail."

Finally, they found a talented triathlon coach, Dan Grieb, who was willing to treat Chris just like any other athlete.

On November 7th, 2020, in Panama City Beach, Florida, Chris set off on his first race. He started off strong but it was not smooth sailing. Tiny, sharp stings raced up his leg when he stepped on a fire anthill. He crashed his bike and battled cramps, fatigue, and exhaustion. But Chris kept going. At 16 hours and 46 minutes, he crossed the finish line and made history by becoming the first person with Down Syndrome to complete an Ironman. He'd swum 2.4 miles, biked 114 miles, and finished strong by running 26.2 miles!

## "I was born a Down Syndrome Kid. Next morning I woke up as an IRONMAN."

Chris firmly believes his abilities are given to him by God. His faith has strengthened him as he has gone on to continue training and completing more races and triathlons. As a public speaker he shares a message of hope, urging people to focus on what they can do and not listen to those who say, "You can't."

# ANN BANCROFT

**BORN 1955**

I get stubborn and dig in when people tell me I can't do something and I think I can. It goes back to my childhood when I had problems in school because I have a learning disability.

Ann Bancroft grew up in Minnesota, USA. She had a natural sense of wanderlust—always seeking out new adventures. Nature was her playground, and she would often come home from school and trade her school uniform for snow pants, then spend the rest of her day exploring. As early as eight years old, she was organizing mini expeditions in her neighborhood. Little did she know, in her adult years she would be doing the same thing but on a much grander scale.

Ann always had a love for athletics and being active, but academics were a challenge. In 7th grade, Ann was diagnosed with Dyslexia—a learning disability that affects reading, writing, and spelling. And back in the 1960s and 1970s, schools didn't have the resources or training to help someone with a learning disability. Despite her challenges, Ann graduated high school, went to college, and became a physical and special education teacher while coaching multiple sports.

From a young age, Ann had aspirations of going all the way to the top of the world, and in 1986, she braved the journey and became the first woman to make it to the North Pole. After her expedition, she created the Ann Bancroft Foundation. Their mission is to "give girls an opportunity to explore their potential and find their place in the world." So many times, Ann was told "no," and she wanted a chance to tell girls that they CAN do it.

Ann's expeditions continued as she ventured to the South Pole, leading a team of four American Women on a 67-day ski trek of 660 miles (1,060 km), making her the first woman to ever make it to each pole. In 1992, she also led the first team of women across Greenland. And in 2001, she did the unthinkable. With polar explorer Liv Arnesan, Ann made it across Antarctica's entire landmass, a total of 1,717 miles (2,747 km)! It took them 94 days to make the journey.

Ann is known as one of the world's most expert polar explorers and a renowned role model for girls and women. What's even better is that she shares her knowledge and love for exploring to help others seek out new horizons and have unique adventures of their own.

# JIM ABBOTT

**BORN 1967**

### Find something you love and go after it with all your heart.

From an early age Jim Abbott showed promise to become a successful athlete.

At eleven years old he threw a no-hitter for his little league team. As a high school senior he was the quarterback for his school's football team. His baseball team won the majority of their games. He consistently hit home runs while averaging at least two strikeouts per inning on the mound. But, no matter how good he was, when people would see Jim's limb difference they would often doubt his athletic talents.

Jim was born without his right hand, yet he always figured out how to do things in his own way. He was most famously known for his time on the mound as a pitcher. When he pitched, he would throw with his left hand and balance the web of his glove on his right forearm. As soon as the ball was thrown, within split seconds, he could slide his left hand into the glove and be ready to field the ball and make a play. Jim consistently proved to be an elite athlete. He not only kept up with his teammates but excelled beyond the average athlete.

In the 1985 Major League Baseball draft, Jim was selected by the Toronto Blue Jays but decided to play for University of Michigan instead. He played for three seasons and was recognized and awarded the James E. Sullivan Award as the top amateur athlete in the country, making him the first ever baseball player to win that award.

In the 1988 Summer Olympic Games Jim pitched for the United States, leading the team to a 5-3 victory over Japan and earning them the Gold Medal.

One year later Jim was drafted to the Anaheim Angels and played with them for four years, until he was drafted by the New York Yankees. On September 4, 1993, Jim made baseball history. In a game against the Cleveland Indians, he achieved the near-impossible when he pitched a no-hitter. Not one player on the opposing team got a hit for the entire game! Only ten Yankees in history have ever thrown a no-hitter.

No matter what team he was playing for, he would draw a crowd and was loved by his fans. He has shown the world what the human spirit is capable of and has taught us to not let our challenges get in the way of what we want to do or who we want to become.

Jim Abbott

# CECE BELL

Cece Bell, the prestigious author and illustrator of *El Deafo* and many other books, has won over the hearts of readers with her storytelling and art.

Thousands of children around the world have come to adore the lovable bunny, Cece, the main character in *El Deafo*. In the book, Cece has a superpower, and her superhero name is—can you guess it? El Deafo! What's awesome is that her superpower isn't from outer space or a secret serum. Cece is deaf, and her disability gives her powers. But it wasn't always empowering.

When Cece was four and half years old, she became ill with bacterial meningitis, and the world around her fell nearly silent. She didn't understand why she suddenly couldn't hear her family, the TV, or all the normal sounds she was used to. She was fitted with hearing aids and once school started, she felt out of place and awkward being the only kid who needed something to help her hear. Not only did she feel different, but she was ashamed of her disability and worried no one would be her friend. As she learned to accept her deafness, she turned it into a superpower and realized that being different didn't make her an outcast.

Cece's childhood was filled with a lot of art. Her love of drawing started as a toddler and Cece's parents cherished and kept her beautiful detailed drawings from when she was young. Her passion stayed with her all the way to adulthood as she majored in art and then published her first book as an author and illustrator in 2003. She has now written and illustrated more than a dozen books and was honored with the famed Newbery Medal Award, recognizing her epic contributions to American children's literature.

In 2014, *El Deafo* gave the world—specifically young readers—a glimpse of life for someone who is Deaf or Hard of Hearing. From social situations to being at school and at home, *El Deafo* shares experiences like kids talking awkwardly loud and slow, introducing her as their "deaf friend," and having to wear a bulky unit that connected to a microphone her teacher wore. Cece's story shows us not only the growing pains of her childhood, but also the acceptance and empowerment of her disability.

Through her writing, Cece has taught everyone that when you share your superpowers, you can make the world a better place and help others find their own superpower.

# JASON DASILVA

**It's hard to know where our stories are going as they are being written. That's the mystery of faith.**

Whether it's on paper, around a campfire, or on a screen, hearing or watching a story unfold can be an extraordinary experience. And some people are born to tell stories—Jason Dasilva is one of those people.

Jason's storytelling began at a young age as he was often found with a camera in his hand capturing the world around him. But, in 2005, everything changed when Jason was diagnosed with primary progressive Multiple Sclerosis.

Multiple Sclerosis mainly affects the brain, spinal, and optic nerves. There are many symptoms including weakened muscles, change in mobility, worsening vision, fatigue, and pain, to name a few.

Jason did everything he could to stay active and healthy in hopes of slowing down or stopping the progression, but there isn't a cure for MS. He was 25 years old and was told he would soon need a cane, then a walker, and eventually a wheelchair.

For seven years, Jason generously pulled back the curtains and filmed his day-to-day life as the disease progressed. He recorded raw and intimate moments in his Emmy-Award winning documentary, *When I Walk*. We're able to watch his first fall to the ground while he was playing volleyball with friends. We follow him to visit family in India, where he turns to ancient medicine practices. We see him struggle to do things like get dressed, feed himself, and travel outside of his apartment. We also watch his discovery of inaccessibility. As Jason started using a wheelchair, he was faced with the reality that he couldn't get into the majority of buildings. Jason hopes for a world that is 100 accessible, and helped create a phone application called AXS Map—a resource that lets users review and rate different venues regarding accessibility. The goal is to cover every major city in the world.

After directing and writing *When I Walk*, he created a sequel titled *When We Walk*, which mainly features life with his son. Jason's film is a love letter to his little boy and something for his son to look back on in the future.

Jason's documented life reminds us of the power of storytelling as he graciously shares his journey with the world—a story that will forever touch hearts and change lives.

# MELISSA STOCKWELL

Being a winner isn't always being at the top of the podium. Being a winner can be overcoming something that comes your way that you don't expect.

From a very young age Melissa Stockwell loved the colors red, white, and blue. She would see them on the American flag and knew that they were more than just random colors thrown together. She understood the meaning of the flag and always had a desire to represent and honor her country.

In 2002 she was commissioned as a 2nd lieutenant in the Army. And in 2004, while deployed in Iraq, Melissa's life changed forever. She was in a routine convoy when her vehicle ran over and detonated a roadside bomb. She was rushed to a local hospital where they amputated her leg, making her the first female to lose a limb in the Iraq war.

While recovering in the hospital, she looked around at her fellow injured soldiers and realized how fortunate she was to be alive. She knew she had the power to choose to find joy in her circumstance.

Melissa turned to sports while she healed and recovered, and was determined to make it to the largest athletic stage in the world—cvthe Paralympics. In 2008 her dreams came true, and in Beijing, China, she competed in swimming. She was appointed to be the flag bearer for the United States and was honored to once again represent her country. After her first Paralympics, she turned her focus to triathlons and went on to compete in many national and international competitions, including the 2016 and 2020 Paralympics. She gracefully competed as a new mother. Her babies were born in 2014 and 2017 and she loved setting an example of tenacity and hard work for her two young children.

As an above-knee amputee, Melissa swims without her prosthetic leg. When she bikes, she uses a custom made bicycle that has what is called a "stump cup" that is fastened to her bike where she can fit her residual limb and pedal with her one sound leg. For running, she wears her famous red, white, and blue stars-and-stripes prosthetic running blade.

Melissa's love of sports goes beyond herself, and in 2011 she co-founded Dare2Tri—a non-profit that has helped numerous athletes succeed in their pursuit of sports.

From a Purple Heart to a Paralympic medal, Melissa inspires everyone she meets. She stands firm in her belief in the power of choice, encouraging everyone to gain the ability to choose positivity and joy.

## WHEELZ'S RECORDS

- first wheelchair back flip
- first wheelchair front flip
- highest ramp jump by wheelchair 60 cm (1 ft 11.6 in)
- longest duration balancing a side wheelie using a wheelchair-18.22 sec
- longest wheelchair ramp jump (21.35 m; 70 ft)
- tallest quarter-pipe drop-in on a wheelchair
- highest wheelchair hand plant (both at 8.4 m; 27 ft 6.7

 # AARON FOTHERINGHAM

**BORN 1991**

**I have wheels stuck to my butt. How can that not be fun!**

Aaron "Wheelz" Fotheringham not only lives life on the edge, but he lives at high speeds, rolling down ginormous ramps and flipping through the air in his wheelchair.

For Wheelz, there's no such thing as living life in a box. He's figured out how to do flips off of mega ramps, do spins and turns, and is continuously finding more extreme ways to spin his wheels. All while making a wheelchair look like the coolest thing ever—because how can you not think it's cool after meeting Wheelz!?

Wheelz grew up in Las Vegas, Nevada. He was born with a condition called Spina Bifida which affects his ability to walk. In his younger years he walked with arm crutches, but once he discovered the freedom and speed he gained from using a wheelchair, he decided to solely use a chair.

Wheelz vividly remembers his first time dropping down into a halfpipe. He was eight years old and his brother encouraged him to get in with the rest of the kids at the skatepark. With some hesitation, Wheelz pushed himself to the edge, shifted his weight forward and wheeled down into the 4 ft. halfpipe and crashed. But, he got up and tried again and again until he mastered one trick at a time.

After many years of practice and hard work, Wheelz made it to the big stage.

In 2010 Wheelz joined the professional action sports team, Nitro Circus. The extreme stunt show travels around the world and performs for millions of people.

Wheelz has made such a grand impact that his wheelchair has been turned into a toy made by a world-renowned toy car company, and you can also find a remote control stunt vehicle of Wheelz in his wheelchair. It may seem like a simple toy to some, but it is a sign of disability inclusion and representation at its finest. Kids can now be found zooming a toy stunt wheelchair around! That's huge!

Wheelz is a true trailblazer for wheelchair motocross and is changing perceptions of disabilities. He shows the world that disabilities might change the way someone does something, but that doesn't mean it isn't absolutely awesome.

# CHELSEA WERNER

**BORN 1992**

**Everyone has challenges in their lives, but it's how you deal with those challenges that makes all the difference!**

People with Down Syndrome typically have low muscle tone and aren't viewed as athletic, but Chelsea Werner's parents went against the grain and enrolled their daughter in gymnastics. Even though it was difficult for Chelsea, she still loved it. She could barely walk across the balance beam and lacked physical strength, but she kept trying. After a few years of training, Chelsea decided to prepare for the Special Olympics.

The Special Olympics is a sporting event for those with intellectual disabilities. The first one took place in 1968 with about one thousand athletes from the USA and Canada. At the most recent Special Olympics, over 7,000 athletes from around 200 countries traveled to Abu Dhabi to participate in over 20 sporting events.

The Special Olympics became a big part of Chelsea's life, but the games didn't occur locally or on a regular basis, which meant she mainly competed with non-disabled athletes. For years she came in last place, but that only motivated her to spend more time training and take competition seriously.

In 2012, Chelsea competed at her first Special Olympics and won! But, she didn't stop there. She attended three more United States Special Olympics, held on to her number one title, and also became a two-time world champion.

Chelsea's successful gymnastics career put her in the limelight, and she caught the attention of H&M, a renowned clothing brand, who asked her to be a part of a campaign. Chelsea immediately fell in love with modeling and, with the help of her parents, started to seek out modeling agencies. Sadly, Chelsea was told over and over that there wasn't a market for a model with Down Syndrome. A couple years later, after seeing a viral video of Chelsea, an agency reached out and hired her. She has now been featured on the cover of Teen Vogue and has been a part of campaigns for Aerie, Tommy Hilfiger, and Target to name a few. Thanks to Chelsea's persistence and grit, people with Down Syndrome have a chance to see themselves represented in the media.

People with Down Syndrome are often stereotyped and told what they can and can't do. Chelsea didn't believe the negative misconceptions. She believed in herself and paved the way for those who want to follow in her footsteps.

# MANI LOVE

**BORN 1985**

*I've never once woken up or went to bed saying, 'God, I wish you didn't make me this way.' I'm happy to be this way; I'm doing everything normal-sized people do, and better.*

Jahmani "Mani Love" Swanson was like most kids—he learned to crawl and then walk. But instead of cuddling with a teddy bear at night, he slept with a basketball. From the moment he first held a basketball, his whole life revolved around the sport. He was a natural, but he also worked hard to develop his talent and proved to be a strong contender as a streetball basketball player in the parks of New York City where he grew up.

When you think of basketball, you picture players towering over anyone less than six feet tall. It is a big person's game and that's pretty much how it's always been. But then, you meet Mani Love—a basketball player who can expertly swoosh, dribble, and square up any opponent brave enough to go against him. And he stands at a whopping 4' 5".

Mani's athletic abilities are smashing the misconceptions people have of those with achondroplasia, also known as a form of dwarfism. He started off on the streets of Harlem and became known as one of the greatest streetballers around. His popularity began in high school as people were intrigued by the little person playing basketball. After college, he was contacted by the Venice Beach Basketball League—a league of twelve teams made up of National Basketball Association players, professional, amateur, and streetball stars. The league gave Mani an even bigger stage to play, and he started to become an internet sensation and famed basketball player.

In 2018, Mani earned a coveted spot on the Harlem Globetrotters as "Hot Shot Swanson." He now travels the world living his dream of being a professional basketball player.

Mani's mom, who was also born with achondroplasia, is his number one fan. She has been able to support Mani in ways no one else could. She would tell him, "Height? What is that? You can't change it so you gotta embrace it." She always encouraged him to be confident and love himself, and he needed that constant reminder because of how often he encountered teasing and bullying.

Aside from basketball, Mani takes time to connect with kids, both with disabilities and non-disabled, to help them advocate for themselves if they are dealing with bullies or feeling different. He inspires them to know that there is no such thing as "can't," and to DREAM BIG!

# UNITED STATES SLED HOCKEY TEAM

Three, two, one . . . BUZZZZZ! Team Norway and USA were tied and sent into overtime at the 2002 Paralympic Winter Games in Salt Lake City, Utah. The suspense made the audience go wild with Norwegian and American flags vigorously waving throughout the stands. It was a fierce competition for the gold. Norway had been reigning champions and the USA was ready to knock them off their pedestal. The overtime clock ran out and the teams were still tied, sending them into an intense shootout—a one-on-one penalty shot competition—against the opposing team's goalie. USA pulled ahead by one goal the score was 4-3. If Norway scored, it would tie the game, again, sending them into another shootout. Norway quickly approached the goal, shifted the puck back and forth, ready to take their final shot. Everyone watched as the puck flew towards the goal and MISSED! Screams erupted and hands clapped into celebratory applause. USA takes the win! They did it—USA Sled Hockey won their first gold. It was their very own miracle on ice as the US hadn't even officially qualified for the Paralympics. They were true underdogs as they were placed in the lowest bracket of the tournament simply out of respect for being the host of that year's Paralympics. Their win was monumental for the sport and had a huge impact on sled hockey as a whole.

Flash forward two decades to the year 2022 at the Paralympic Winter Games in Beijing, China. Would the US sled hockey team's winning streak come to an end? The team's unity and skills were a force to be reckoned with as they took to the ice and defended their number one title. Five goals were scored against Canada, making the final score 5-0. It was a strong shutout. USA took home a gold for the fourth Paralympic Games games in a row! It was their fifth gold overall.

Sled hockey is an inclusive adaptive sport for a variety of disabilities to enjoy, whether someone has a limb difference, is a bilateral leg amputee, or paralysis. It made its Paralympic debut in 1994, but was developed in the early 1960s at a rehabilitation center in Stockholm, Sweden. It is a fast paced, high energy game played very similarly to hockey, but each player uses two sticks and sits in a sled with two hockey skate blades attached to the bottom. The two sticks have metal picks on the end of the handles, used to navigate and propel forward on the ice. It takes a lot of balance and control to stay upright and maneuver the sled.

With the support of major groups, such as the National Hockey League, USA Hockey, and Challenged Athletes Foundation, people are learning about and becoming fans of the sport as it gains momentum in popularity. With the Paralympic movement in full swing, more and more younger athletes are looking up to Paralympians and are inspired to get on the ice and play sled hockey.

## GUINNESS WORLD RECORD

The most Winter Paralympic para ice hockey gold medals is 5, by the USA in 2002, 2010, 2014, 2018 and 2022.

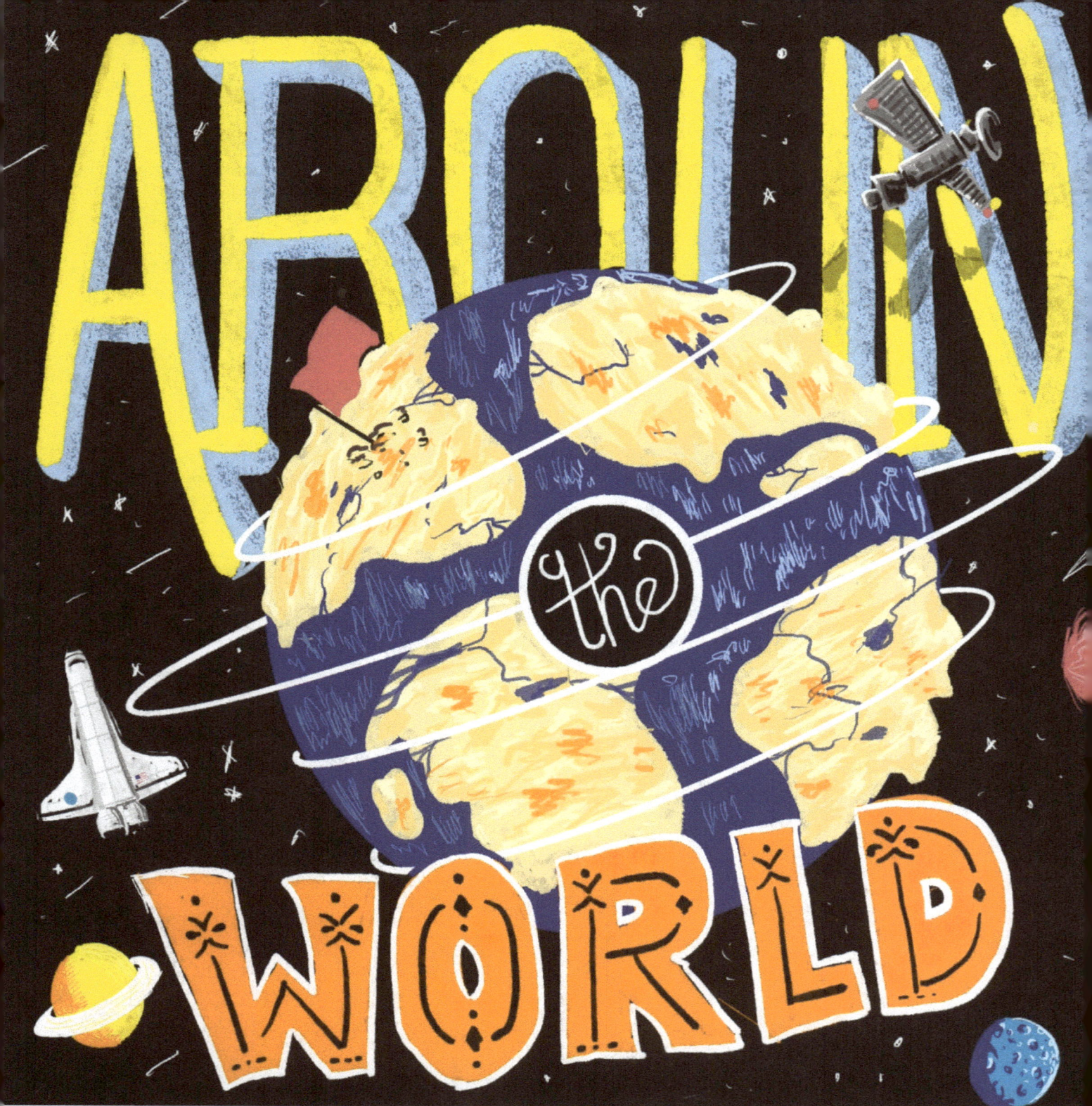

# A LOOK AT THE PEOPLE AROUND THE WORLD WHO REPRESENT!

Dylan Alcott

Mayumi Narita

Claire Cunninghan

Hermon & Heroda Berhane

Jean Dominique Bauby

Mary Verghese

Christy Brown

Gabriela Brimmer

Natasha Lambert

# DYLAN ALCOTT

 AUSTRALIA

=BORN=
**1990**

**"...just because you are disabled, it's not a life sentence; your life's not over, there's still so many things that you can do to get out there and live a happy and successful life."**

Dylan Alcott has only known life with a disability. He was born with a tumor wrapped around his spine, causing his paralysis. When he was young he dealt with bullies, endured common stigmas and people's pity surrounding the disability community. He hated his disability, and especially being different. But as he grew older, he started to believe the people who loved him and knew his life was worth living.

As a teenager, Dylan proved to be a superstar athlete. At age fifteen Dylan joined the Australian national wheelchair basketball team and won a bronze at the world championship. Two years later, Dylan was the youngest member of the 2008 Paralympic team and they took home a gold. In 2010, at the next world championships, Australia came back stronger than ever and claimed their title as number one in the whole world.

After many years of wheelchair basketball, Dylan switched gears and turned his focus to wheelchair tennis. His natural athletic abilities, determination, and hard work earned him multiple Paralympic Gold Medals. He also won 15 Grand Slam singles events and 8 Grand Slam doubles titles. Grand Slam tennis tournaments are the world's most prestigious professional tennis tournaments.

Dylan wins tournaments not only because he works hard and loves the sport, but "to change perceptions so people with disabilities live the lives that they deserve to live."

Today, Dylan will confidently tell you he is proud of his disability and loves his life. He is achieving his dreams and helping others to do the same. Young athletes look to him as a real life superhero as he leads the Dylan Alcott Foundation, which strives to "help young Australians with disabilities gain confidence, fulfill their potential, and achieve their dreams." He also started an accessible and inclusive music festival, Ability Fest, to help raise money for sporting equipment and scholarships at esteemed education institutions, as well as mentoring programs. He is always striving to smash negative perceptions of people with disabilities and works hard to advocate for their needs.

 # MAYUMI NARITA

JAPAN

=BORN=
**1970**

> "Sports have an amazing power that cannot be expressed in words."

Mayumi Narita's disability has not gotten in the way of what she loves to do. She was born with myelitis, which is an inflammation of the spinal cord, causing paralysis of her legs. In her twenties she found her place in the pool, and discovered joy and empowerment in her body despite not being able to use her legs.

At the 1996 Paralympic Games in Atlanta, Georgia, Mayumi's swim cap was perfectly snug on her head and her goggles fit just right. She proudly sported the Japanese flag as she took her place in the pool. The buzzer sounded and she exploded down her lane, meticulously reaching through each stroke and taking a breath as her face emerged from the water. She gracefully, yet speedily, glided through the pool and pulled ahead of all her opponents. Her hand reached out first place was a mere split second away. She touched the wall and was instantly declared the winner. GOLD! That was the beginning of Mayumi's epic Paralympic career. In 2004, at the Paralympic Games in Athens Greece, she set six world records, won seven gold medals, and one bronze. She swam for a total of twenty-five years at the Paralympic level, setting multiple records, taking home fifteen gold medals, two silver, and three bronze. She is known as the "Queen of the Water" and has been deemed to be one of the greatest Paralympic swimmers of all time.

The 2020 Paralympic Games, held in her cherished homeland of Japan, Mayumi competed one last time. She was fifty-one years old! Even though it was the end of her Paralympic journey, her love for swimming will never fade. She is currently giving back to the swimming community and turning her attention to future Paralympians, helping them to achieve their dreams.

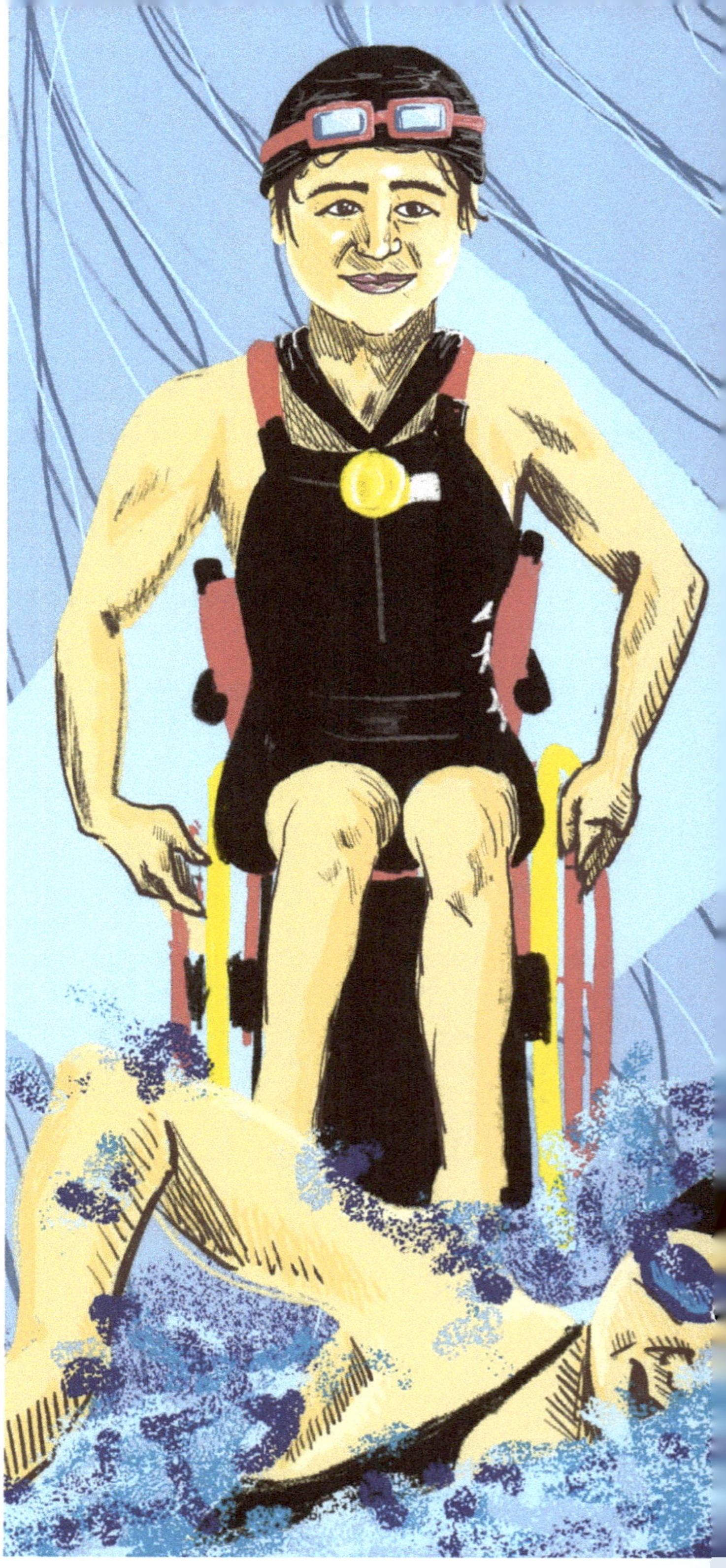

# CLAIRE CUNNINGHAM

**SCOTLAND**

===BORN===
**1977**

Traditional dance technique and performance doesn't always work for someone who has a disability, but that hasn't stopped Claire Cunningham from taking the stage as a dancer.

Claire was born with osteoporosis—a skeletal disorder that causes bones to become weak and brittle. The bones can become so brittle that a fall or even mild stress such as bending over or coughing, can result in bone fractures.

Claire uses arm crutches as a mobility aid, as well as part of her choreography. She balances on top of the crutches and sometimes even balances *them* on top of *her*. She even uses them as props to create visuals on stage. One of her most famous pieces, *Guide Gods* has moments of her tiptoeing, with her crutches, on fragile and dainty tea cups. Each cup represents a person with a disability, and in her performance she shares a lived experience from each person she connected with. She sometimes incorporates singing and live music into her dance numbers, as she originally trained to be a singer before she started dancing.

Claire's desire to perform is a creative outlet and a need for expression, but the more she connects with people, the more she realizes that her art is a sense of activism. She is inspiring younger artists to follow in her footsteps, and break the mold of what a typical dancer looks like and how they move. She also advocates for theater spaces to be more inclusive and welcome more people who have disabilities.

Claire's ability to push creative boundaries has led her to gain a renowned reputation all around the world as a choreographer and artist.

pg.34

# HERMON & HERODA BERHANE

ERITREA

=BORN=
**1983**

### "Diversity is not a trend."

In the war torn country of Eritrea, in Eastern Africa, lived identical twins Hermon and Heroda Berhane. To escape the danger of their homeland, their mother moved them to the United Kingdom. Around that same time, seven year old Hermon and Heroda mysteriously went deaf on the same exact day. Being so young, they didn't understand why, so suddenly, they couldn't hear the sounds they were used to. As time passed, they grieved and learned to accept their new path in life. They started to learn British Sign Language to communicate and began to celebrate their differences.

Their love of fashion and desire to see positive representation in the media has driven them to the path of being a part of the modeling, acting, and fashion industry. They hope to see more diversity within these spaces.

Unfortunately, they have experienced discrimination and faced difficulties in pursuing a career within those three passions. They are often looked down upon because of the lack of awareness around those who are deaf and hard of hearing. Still, they keep pushing forward and want people to be more aware of and understand the deaf community.

Their famous travel-meets-fashion blog, *Being Her*, is direct proof of their determination to have a voice and for their aspirations to be heard. They bravely share their journey with beaming smiles, fierce poses, and fashion you can't help but wish was your own personal closet. They see their disability as an advantage and don't look at it as a challenge they need to overcome.

# JEAN DOMINIQUE BAUBY

 FRANCE  **BORN** 1952 - **DIED** 1997

Jean Dominique Bauby was a successful, well known and charismatic journalist who worked as Editor in Chief for the famous French magazine, ELLE. When he was forty-five years old, he had a stroke that caused him to be in a "locked in" state, also known as Locked-In Syndrome—a rare neurological disorder where one is completely paralyzed except for the muscles in their eyes. Even though Jean was locked in a body he couldn't use he was still fully aware, with an intact, brilliant mind.

Before his stroke, Jean signed a contract to write a memoir to give people a chance to read about his fascinating life.

With the help from Claude Mendibil—a ghostwriter and freelance book editor—Jean wrote the entire memoir, *The Diving Bell and the Butterfly*. Claude would recite the alphabet and when Jean blinked his left eye she would notate the letter. They worked for three hours a day, six days a week, and Jean blinked approximately 200,000 times!

In 1997, two days after the publication of his memoir, Jean died of pneumonia. He never knew how beloved his book had become or that it was a number one national bestseller. Ten years later, in 2007, his life was turned into a movie, *The Diving Bell and the Butterfly*. The film was so successful it was nominated for four Academy Awards.

# MARY VERGHESE

 **INDIA**   **BORN** **1925** – **DIED** **1986**

"My disability is not a punishment by God. Rather, it is my greatest asset as a doctor."

Physical rehabilitation in India would not be what it is today without Mary Vergese.

Ever since she was a little girl, Mary had aspirations of becoming a doctor. She was often recognized for her intelligence, worked hard on her academics, and always pursued her dreams of working in the medical field.

Upon graduating medical school, Mary got into a car accident and became paralyzed. She had never seen anyone practice medicine from a wheelchair and fell into a deep despair, wondering how she would continue to do what she loved.

With the help and motivation from fellow doctors, she decided to not give up and found ways to treat patients from a chair. She started with performing surgery on the hands of people with leprosy. Practicing medicine again gave her the confidence she needed to move forward.

Mary quickly developed a rapport among the patients with disabilities, and gave them hope and meaning in their lives. She also discovered ways to improve mobility aids for people who needed them.

Upon experiencing her own rehabilitation, Mary understood the importance of helping patients regain their physical independence, which led to her integral involvement in pioneering the first rehabilitation center in India. Her efforts in starting the rehab center have positively changed and are still changing many lives. She always encouraged her patients to find ways to be independent, and taught them that life does not end because of a disability.

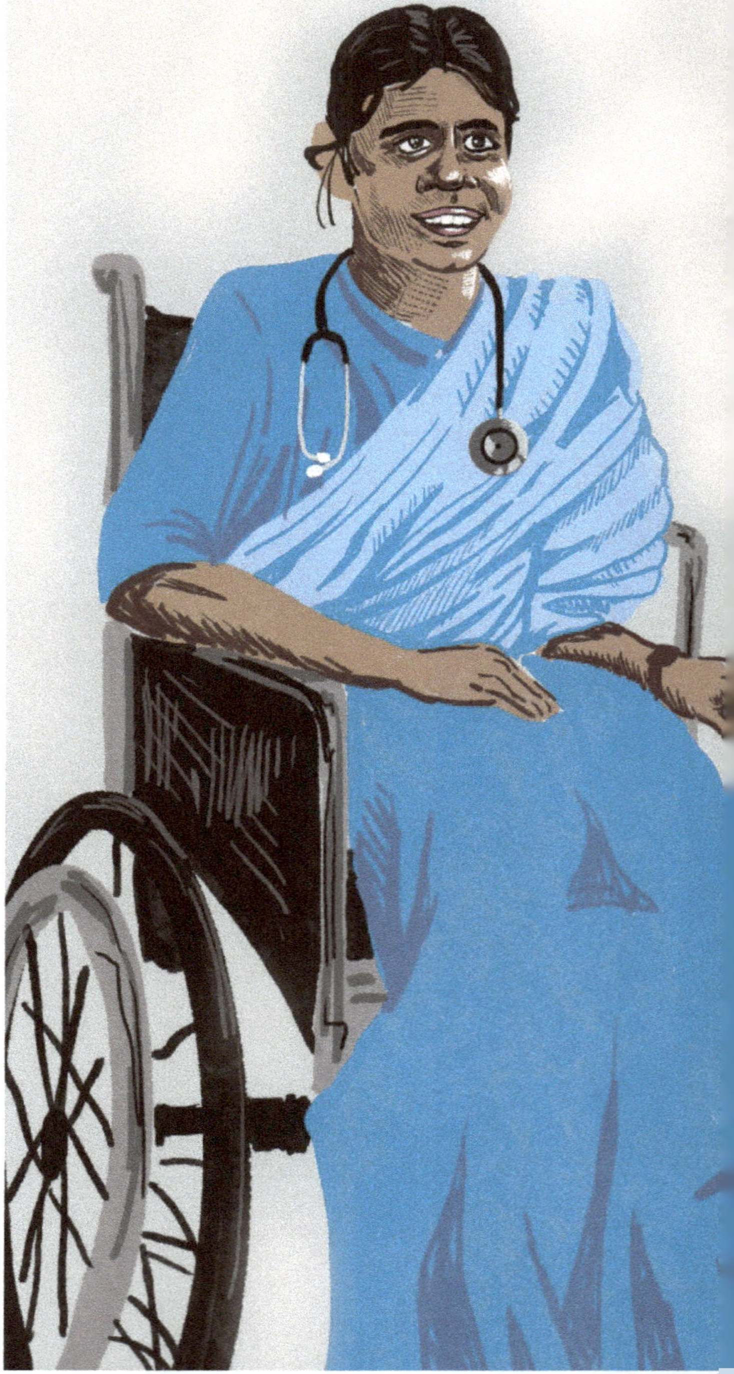

# CHRISTY BROWN

**IRELAND**  **BORN** **1932** — **DIED** **1981**

On June 5, 1932, in Dublin, Ireland, Christy Brown was born. He was one of 13 siblings and born with cerebral palsy—a group of neurological disorders that affect one's muscles, physical movement, balance, and posture. Christy was mostly paralyzed but could control his left leg, foot, and toes.

Despite the doctor's recommendation to send him away to live in a hospital full time, his parents were determined to raise him at home. When he was young, his family didn't know if he would be able to use any part of his body until one day, he picked up a piece of chalk with his left foot and started to write letters on the floor.

As Christy grew older, he mastered the use of his left foot and began to paint and wrzite. His art was full of color and energy, and he had a lyrical way of writing stories and poetry. He quickly started to become popular for being a naturally gifted writer and painter. One would never guess that his paintings were done by someone who used their foot or that his writings were typed out with his toes.

As an adult he published his first book, *My Left Foot*, and became a literary sensation which began his rise to fame. His book was an international bestseller and was translated into multiple languages.

Christy is proof that talent can come about in many different ways, and his art and writings will forever be a gift to our world and a testament of his creative mind.

# GABRIELA BRIMMER

**MEXICO**

**BORN** **DIED**
**1947 — 2000**

Gabriela Brimmer is a Mexican-Jewish activist and gifted writer who was born with cerebral palsy—a group of neurological disorders that affect one's muscles, physical movement, balance, and posture. Gaby was able to control her left foot and toes, and communicated with either a typewriter or alphabet board.

When Gaby was a teenager, she attended a school exclusively for disabled teens. The education she received was not equal to her non-disabled peers, yet she knew she was just as capable of it. Her body had limited abilities but that didn't mean she wasn't intelligent. She fought for her right to attend public school and eventually won the battle, opening a door for others to follow.

The more Gaby communicated, the more she realized the importance of having a voice. She wanted to be a mouthpiece for the disability community. But stories like hers were unheard of in that day; it was not common for people with disabilities to speak up and share their lives with the world. Today, stories of people with disabilities are now widely revered and even make their way to bestseller lists, but back in Gaby's time it was not as common. Still, she bravely published her first book—*Gaby Brimmer An Autobiography in Three Voices*. Gaby believed her life and story mattered and was worth being told.

In 1989 Gaby fought for the injustices of the disability community, and founded the Association for the Rights of People With Motor Disabilities. The organization provides resources for counseling, medical, and psychological services, and has helped countless people throughout Mexico.

Because of Gaby's bravery and determination, she has been able to become a pioneer—opening doors for rights in education, disability services, and even paving the way for others to tell their own stories.

# ⚓ NATASHA LAMBERT

 UNITED KINGDOM   BORN 1997

*"I hope to encourage other disabled people that sailing is possible no matter what your ability. If I can do it, anyone can!"*

Natasha Lambert is from Cowes, Isle of Wight, the home of British Sailing. She loves the smell of the sea and the feeling of the wind as it rushes past her face. She also loves the independence she gains from being able to control the sails all by herself. The way Natasha sails is a little different from the average sailor. She uses a sip-puff system that allows her to use her breath and tongue to control the rudder and the angle of the sails, and her tongue can flick a switch and change the boat to auto-steering. She uses this method because she has quadriplegic cerebral palsy—a condition which affects the control of her arms and legs. Being able to utilize the sip-puff technology has opened huge doors for sailing and has been perfect for her!

Natasha's love for sailing began when she was nine years old. She loved being at sea but wanted to be more than just a passenger. At age fourteen, after years of training, Natasha fulfilled her dream of becoming a skipper on a boat. She recalls, "I had never ever been able to do anything on my own. I always had someone helping me. Control and freedom at last!"

When Natasha was twenty-three years old, she helped chart a risky, yet exciting, course—a nearly 3,000 mile Transatlantic journey. While family and friends rooted her on, she and a crew of five crossed from Gran Canaria to Saint Lucia in eighteen days and twenty-one hours. On that day, she became the first person to sail across the Atlantic using sip-puff technology.

Natasha shares her love of sailing through her charity, the Miss Isle School of Sip and Puff Sailing. She makes it possible for other young sailors to take sip and puff sailing trips and hopes to help people to know that sailing is for everyone.

# ROLLETTES

**"If you don't think I can do it, I'm gonna let that fuel me to get it done even better."**

In 2012, Chelsie Hill had the brilliant idea of creating a dance team, but not just any dance team—one where they dance while using a wheelchair.

Two years earlier, during her senior year of high school, Chelsie was in a car accident and became paralyzed from the waist down. Growing up, dance was a major part of her life and something she cherished. Now that she used a wheelchair she knew she wouldn't be able to walk again, but that didn't mean her dancing days were over.

Her new mission in life was to figure out how to dance in her own way and to bring along as many people as she could.

When Chelsie dances, she doesn't feel different. Dance gives her a sense of freedom and a way to express herself. She wanted to share that joy with others, so she moved to Los

Angeles to find other women who were interested in dancing, leading to the founding of the wheelchair dance team—Rollettes. When they dance they are full of energy and life as they feel the music through their bodies. They move across the stage in their wheelchairs with great musicality and rhythm. The dancers prove that they are not bound to their disability or their chairs rather, they use them as mobility aids to create movement and art.

Once the Rollettes were established, they dreamed even bigger and The Rollettes Experience was born. The event is for women of all ages and disabilities and is full of dancing, mentoring, and empowerment. Attendees travel from all around the world to connect with a community that helps them know they are not alone.

The Rollettes are more than a dance team, they are trailblazers, shifting perspectives and changing lives for the better.

# EDUARDO GARCIA

**A meal is not just what we eat, but a rich story of who we are!**

In Montana, USA, lives an avid outdoorsman, active athlete, and talented chef named Eduardo Garcia. From a young age, Eduardo loved living on the abundant land of Montana.

At age 15, Eduardo's relationship with food began when he got a job in a kitchen. He found purpose in creating an experience through cooking. After high school, Eduardo thrived in culinary school. Upon graduation he became a professional chef on a yacht and traveled the world. For over a decade, he connected with multiple cultures which helped him gain a diverse palate and global influence in his cuisine.

In 2011, Eduardo was out hunting when he came across a dead bear in a metal barrel. When he touched the bear with the metal blade of his knife, he connected with a live wire hidden under the bear. Eduardo was instantly electrocuted with 2,400 volts, leaving him barely alive. With the will to survive, Eduardo walked his trauma-ridden body three miles to the nearest road where he was found and rushed to the hospital.

Eduardo underwent 18 surgeries, including the amputation of his left hand, removal of four ribs, as well as parts of the major muscle groups in his legs and torso, followed by ten months of intensive scalp reconstruction.

After a long and arduous recovery, Eduardo had to relearn how to do everything with his one natural hand and a prosthetic hand. He wasn't sure how to cut food or hold a pan and stir, but he was determined to figure it out. Incredibly, he discovered that he could reach directly into a scalding hot pan to stir food or flip bacon with his prosthetic hook. He may have lost his arm, but he gained a whole new kitchen utensil!

Eduardo returned to being an avid outdoorsman and also a successful chef. He is known as the "bionic chef" and has a flourishing food business called MONTANA MEX. He also loves to give back to the disability community, as he donates a portion of the proceeds from his business to Challenged Athletes Foundation, an organization that uses sports to support veterans, amputees, and other physically challenged kids and adults.

Eduardo may live his life a little differently than he expected, but his zest for life is as flavorful as the food he creates.

 # TEMPLE GRANDIN

**BORN 1947**

> If I could snap my fingers and be non-autistic, I would not. Autism is a part of who I am.

Back in the 1950s, autism was widely misunderstood. Doctors would often advise parents to put their children in mental institutions and sometimes misdiagnose them with brain damage.

Though Temple Grandin is on the autism spectrum, her mother refused to listen to the doctors and found people who were willing to help.

Temple did not speak until she was four. She would have autistic meltdowns and had a hard time learning and keeping up with her peers. Her mother eventually enrolled her in a private school where they would nurture her intelligence. Some teachers saw Temple's potential and were amazed with her intelligence. Her autism causes her to think in pictures, which helped her to become a great animal scientist and see things in a way others couldn't.

When Temple was a teenager, she went to her aunt's ranch and discovered her ability to connect with animals. She watched, studied, and observed their behavior. After that visit, she continued on the path of studying animals and attended Arizona State University for a doctorate in animal science. She excelled in her studies and is now renowned for her discoveries and methods in the cattle and ranching world.

Because she was female and people didn't understand her disability, she was often turned away from ranches and slaughterhouses. But, Temple was tenacious. Despite the lack of inclusion, she kept fighting for ways to get back into the places where she was rejected to study and gather research.

Temple is known worldwide for her activism and extensive exploration of animal behavior. She is highly involved in the humane treatment of livestock and is an author of more than sixty scientific papers. Her designs have transformed the livestock industry and are used across the United States.

Temple is also a passionate advocate for the disability community—writing books and speaking to audiences around the world. When someone on the spectrum tells her they want to follow in her footsteps as a disability advocate, she encourages them to do so but also motivates them to find their talents and pursue those as well. She knows that being on the autism spectrum makes her who she is, but is not her entire identity.

Temple is recognized as one of the most influential people in the world and will forever be revered as a brilliant scientist and activist.

# MIKE COOTS

**BORN 1981**

Life doesn't end when you become limbless. It's really just the beginning of a new, exciting chapter of life.

On the tropical island of Hawaii, there lives a zealous surfer, diver, world renowned photographer, and shark activist. Being in the ocean is where he feels most at home, and he is considered a crusader for the conservation of sharks. Because of his love for sharks, one might have a hard time believing that he is a shark attack survivor.

When Mike was eighteen years old, he went to the beach and paddled his surfboard out beyond the break to catch some waves. Only five minutes into his surf, a tiger shark bit down on his right leg, and Mike instantly became a below-knee amputee.

As soon as the doctors cleared Mike to go back in the water, he went straight to the place he knew best—the ocean. He began to surf again and took on the learning curve of adapting to a prosthetic leg. It was a challenge, but he wasn't going to let his limb loss stop him from doing what he loved. He kept surfing!

Mike believes in and hopes for the coexistence of sharks and humans, and is dedicating his life to advocacy. In 2010, he was a large part of the efforts to ban the possession of shark fins in Hawaii. Fortunately, other states in the USA followed suit.

Mike's activism can also be found in his art as a photographer. He has a way of beautifying sharks rather than the usual villainization. When you see his photographs you'll find gentle, peaceful creatures. Sometimes they even look like they are smiling! Imagine that, a smiling shark, like it's straight out of a cartoon.

Mike isn't only an advocate for sharks and the ecosystem, but also young adaptive athletes. He strives to be a mentor for others who have disabilities. He says, "It was worth losing a limb just for that alone . . . to help other amputees and kids that are dealing with limb loss." He often travels to Southern California to teach kids with disabilities how to surf. He is active with the Challenged Athletes Foundation (just like Eduardo Garcia!) and loves helping young kids with limb differences.

# LEX GILLETTE

**BORN 1984**

**Be an agent of positive change. Initiate, articulate, and motivate.**
*FLY!* BY LEX GILLETTE

Lex Gillette grew up in North Carolina, USA and had a wonderful but out-of-the-ordinary childhood. When he was eight-years-old he went blind due to recurrent retinal detachment.

Growing up blind was not easy for Lex, but his mom was a strong support system for him, especially when he had to endure ten surgeries and learn how to grow accustomed to the loss of his vision.

Lex loved sports and would often play basketball for hours with the hoop that hung on the backside of his bedroom door. He got so good that he could stand anywhere in his room and sink the ball in the net. To know whether or not he made the ball into the basket, he fastened a safety pin to the bottom of his net so the ball wouldn't fall out. If he missed, he'd hear the ball thump on the floor, and if he heard nothing he knew the ball was safe inside the net he'd made the shot! This was just the beginning of Lex's determination to succeed and figure out how to do things in his own way.

In high school, during a mandatory fitness test, Lex had to do a standing long jump. He firmly planted his feet, swung his arms, and hoisted himself forward. He flew through the air and landed at nine feet and eight inches. Lex's physical education teacher immediately recognized his superb athletic abilities and told him about the Paralympics, something Lex had never even heard of. Lex soon started to train and at nineteen years old, in 2004, he made his Paralympic debut and won silver in the long jump. Since then, he has become a five-time Paralympic medalist, a four-time long jump world champion, and an 18-time national champion.

Lex is also a musician who loves to sing and play the piano. And besides track and field, Lex enjoys beep baseball. Just imagine playing a form of baseball with a blindfold on and a ball that beeps. Now that takes skill!

Lex has a vision unlike any other and is a highly sought-after motivational speaker. He shares his inspiring story on stages all over the world and believes that whether it's big or small, everyone has a vision. Go after what you want and believe in yourself. Be like Lex, close your eyes, and take a giant leap of faith!

# MANDY HARVEY

**BORN 1988**

*If I take back any of the bumps, bruises, or scrapes I've been through, I wouldn't be the same person.*

Mandy Harvey spent her childhood dreaming of becoming a professional musician. Her life was filled with melodies, harmonies, and rhythm. Her passion led her to pursue a career in music but at nineteen-years-old, that dream fell silent along with the world around her.

During Mandy's freshman year of college, she became profoundly deaf, caused by Ehlers-Danlos syndrome, which is a connective tissue disorder.

Mandy experienced deep depression as she grieved and struggled with her newfound barriers. She didn't pick up a guitar, play the piano, or sing. She admits there was a period of time when she gave up, until one day her father finally convinced her to pick up a guitar again. As she strummed, she felt the vibration against her body and realized music was still there—she just had to figure out how it fit into her new world. At that moment, hope started to return. She soon found her voice again and was able to produce the same gorgeous sound she had been making her entire life. An added bonus was her new knowledge of American Sign Language. She would mesmerize audiences with her lyrical signs while she sang. After dedicating many hours, days, and months to practicing, she knew she was ready to take the stage again, but not just any stage.

In 2017, Mandy Harvey stepped onto one of the largest stages in the world—America's Got Talent—and sang in front of millions of people. In hopes of inspiring at least ONE person, she sang one of her own songs with lyrics about trying over and over again

Mandy finished her song and the celebrity judges clapped and celebrated her outstanding performance. They not only praised her, but one of the most respected judges, Simon Cowell, gave her his only golden buzzer. She was showered in shiny gold confetti while tears of joy streamed down her face. She was sent straight to the live show which takes place right before the finale. She did it! She broke through barriers and showed the world what she could do. She pursued her dreams despite all the roadblocks she faced. She is now a touring musician, has numerous albums, and inspires millions of people to keep on trying and to follow their dreams.

# HUNTER WOODHALL

**BORN 1999**

**It's not about proving the disbelievers wrong, but proving the people who believe in you right.**

Did you know that the Paralympic movement is in full force?!

The Paralympic Games are for athletes with physical disabilities and visual impairments. They started back in 1960 with 400 athletes from 23 countries in Rome, Italy. At the 2020 Tokyo games, there were over 4,000 athletes from 163 countries! The Paralympics have introduced us to sports like sitting volleyball, wheelchair tennis, wheelchair basketball, and sled hockey. People around the world are watching and following athletes, learning about adaptive sports, and getting excited for the games that run parallel to the Olympic Games, hence the name 'Paralympics.' One specific athlete to watch for is Hunter Woodhall.

Hunter was born with fibular hemimelia, a condition where fibula bones never form or are too short. At eleven months old, both of his legs were amputated below the knee.

Hunter is now a track star, online sensation, and public figure. He is changing perceptions and the way people view disabilities, specifically limb differences, just by being present and visible on social media. People gravitate toward Hunter's infectious personality and love learning about how he does life as a bilateral amputee with two prosthetic legs. What people are finding is that he's not all that different from you or me. Yes, he can walk on LEGOS™ without so much as a flinch and take a scooter to the shin without a scratch, but all in all, he's a pretty normal guy living a happy and fulfilling life.

In middle school, Hunter joined the track team so he could run with his friends, but, when it came to racing he wasn't always the leader of the pack. He could tell that people cheered for him simply for showing up, but he wanted more than that. Hunter started to take training more seriously and became stronger and faster. His hard work and determination to become better took him to the 2015 World Championships, winning silver for the 400m and bronze for the 200m. He also became the Utah State High School Champion and the record holder for the 400m and 200m.

When it was time for Hunter to go to college, he was rejected by multiple schools even though he was one of the fastest runners in the country. There had never been a double amputee in the National Collegiate Athletic Association, and they weren't willing to take a chance on him. Fortunately, the University of Arkansas knew that Hunter would be an asset to their track and field team and offered him a scholarship, making him the first ever double amputee to earn a Division I athletic scholarship.

Hunter is now one of the fastest runners in the world and can be found competing at the most prestigious track and field events. And to think, some thought he would never walk. But with the use of prosthetic legs, a wobbly walk turned into solid steps, a slow jog turned into long strides and those strides turned into record-breaking sprints!

Hunter didn't just become an athlete—he became a champion!

# FURTHER READING & RESOURCES

**You've just learned about 30 amazing people! Want to know more about them and ways to support them? Check out these resources.**

Some books, documentaries or movies might contain mature content and may need to be screened by an adult before reading or watching.

### AARON FOTHERINGHAM
Read: *Wheelz On the Moon* (*Adventures of Mike Believe*) by Michael Dolman and Aaron Wheelz Fotheringham *Wheelz* by Steven C. Fotheringham
Browse: aaronfotheringham.com

### ALI STROKER
Read: *The Chance to Fly* by Ali Stroker
*Ali and the Sea Stars* by Ali Stroker
Browse: alistroker.com

### ANN BANCROFT
Read: *No Horizon Is So Far: Two Women and Their Historic Journey across Antarctica* by Liv Arneson, Ann Bancroft and Cheryl Dahle
Browse: annbancroftfoundation.org

### CECE BELL
Read: *El Deafo* by Cece Bell
Watch: *El Deafo* (Apple TV)
Browse: cecebell.wordpress.com

### CHELSEA WERNER
Browse: chelseaworldchampion.com

### CHRIS NIKIC
Read: *1% Better* by Chris Nikic
Browse: chrisnikic.com

### CHRISTY BROWN
Read: *My Left Foot* by Christy Brown
Watch: *My Left Foot*

### CLAIRE CUNNINGHAM
Browse: clairecunningham.co.uk

### DYLAN ALCOTT
Read: *Able: Gold Medals, Grand Slams and Smashing Glass Ceilings* by Dylan Alcott
Browse: dylanalcottfoundation.com.au

### EDUARDO GARCIA
Watch: *Charged*
Big Sky Kitchen With Eduardo Garcia
Browse: chefeduardo.com

### ERIK WEIHENMAYER
Read: *No Barriers: A Blind Man's Journey to Kayak the Grand Canyon (The Young Adult Adaptation)* by Erik Weihenmayer
*Touch the Top of the World: A Blind Man's Journey*

*to Climb Farther Than the Eye Can See* by Erik Weihenmayer
Watch: *The Weight of Water*
*Welcome to Earth (Disney+)*
Browse: erikweihenmayer.com

## GABRIELA BRIMMER
Read: *Gaby Brimmer: An Autobiography in Three Voices* by Gaby Brimmer and Elena Poniatowska
Watch: *Gaby: A True Story*

## HERMON AND HERODA BERHANE
Browse: beinghermonheroda.com

## HUNTER WOODHALL
Browse: paralympic.org/hunter-woodhall
Watch: youtube.com/@Taraandhunter

## JAMES CASTLE
Read: *Silent Days, Silent Dreams* by Allen Say
Browse: jamescastle.com

## JASON DASILVA
Watch: *When I Walk, When We Walk*

## JIM ABBOTT
Read: *Imperfect* by Jim Abbott

## JEAN DOMINIQUE BAUBY
Read: *The Diving Bell and the Butterfly* by Jean Dominique Bauby
Watch: *The Diving Bell and the Butterfly*

## JESSICA COX
Read: *Disarm Your Limits: The Flight Formula to Lift You to Success and Propel You to the Next Horizon* by Jessica Cox
Watch: *Right Footed*
Browse: jessicacox.com

## LEX GILLETTE
Read: *Fly!: Find Your Own Wings And Soar Above Life's Challenges* by Lex Gillette
Browse: lexgillette.com

## MANDY HARVEY
Read: *Sensing the Rhythm: Finding My Voice in a World Without Sound* by Mandy Harvey
Browse: mandyharveymusic.com

## MANI LOVE
Browse: harlemglobetrotters.com/world-tour/roster/hot-shot/eaglescry.net/2343/sports/fulfilling-hoop-dreams-the-mani-love-story/

## MARY VERGHESE
Read: *Take My Hands The Remarkable Story Of Dr Mary Verghese* by Dorthy Clarke Wilson

## MELISSA STOCKWELL
Read: *The Power of Choice* by Melissa Stockwell
Browse: melissastockwell.com

## MIKE COOTS
Browse: Sharksbymikecoots.com

## NATASHA LAMBERT
Browse: missisle.com

## ROLLETTES
Browse: rollettesdance.com

## TEMPLE GRANDIN
Read: *The Autistic Brain: Helping Different Kinds of Minds Succeed* by Temple Grandin, Richard Panek *The Girl Who Thought in Pictures: The Story of Dr. Temple Grandin (Amazing Scientists)* by Julia Finley Mosca

*Who is Temple Grandin?* by Patricia Brennan Demuth
*Visual Thinking: The Hidden Gifts of People Who Think in Pictures, Patterns, and Abstractions*
by Temple Grandin PhD, Andrea Gallo
Watch: *Temple Grandin*
Browse: templegrandin.com

## US SLED HOCKEY TEAM
Read: *Hockey's Hidden Gods: The Untold Story of a Paralympic Miracle on Ice* by S. C. Megale
Watch: *Ice Warriors*

## PARALYMPIC GAMES
Read: *What Are the Paralympic Games?* by Gail Herman
Read: *A Sporting Chance: How Ludwig Guttmann Created the Paralympic Games*
by Lori Alexander and Allan Drummond
Watch: *Rising Phoenix*

For more books like ours, check out:
*I Am Not a Label* by Carrie Burnell
*Tenacious: Fifteen Adventures Alongside Disabled Athletes* by Patty Cisneros Prevo

**Organizations to support:**
Annbancroftfoundation.org
Challengedathletes.org
Classroomchampions.org
Dare2Tri.org
Dylanalcottfoundation.com.au
Jordanthomasfoundation.org
Nobarriersusa.org
Paralympic.org
Shrinerschildrens.org
Specialolympics.org

# INDEX

# ACKNOWLEDGEMENTS

This book would not have been possible without our publisher, Motina Books. From the beginning, Diane has believed in us, and her faith in our success has never wavered. She champions our advocacy and storytelling and we are so lucky to have her in our corner.

My husband, Michael, has not only supported Hunter as he has adapted and grown into his disability, but he has stood by our advocacy, big ideas, and dreams. He also listens while I read aloud my endless word manuscripts and chatter about my plans and goals. Thanks, babe. Thank you for always being my rock.

To Cade and Logan, you are a bright light in my life. You have been so patient as Hunter and I have pushed through this journey of publishing. I love you guys so much! I hope you will cherish my books forever. And to my in-laws, mom, and close friends—thank you for all your excitement and support! I love you!

The beta and sensitivity readers have really combed through each bio and I couldn't have done this book without them. They came through with flying colors! Ryan Rae Harbuck, Mary and Ryan Mecham, Michelle Hu, and Sandy Kreps—thank you!!

Debbie Despain—my forever editor and the reason I use "em dashes." You are more than my editor, you are my friend and your support has kept me motivated. Thank you for everything and for dealing with my zero knowledge of punctuation. Kidding not kidding.

Brant and the whole Day family. First of all, Brant, you were born to create art. So, for that I am incredibly grateful our paths have crossed and that you were willing to take a chance on this book. Bravo on your very first illustrated book! It will always be a treasure to us. And Amber and kids, thank you for being a generous and kind family. You guys are awesome!

To our wonderful, unique, and beautiful disability community, specifically everyone who was named in this book. How could we have done this without your courage, tenacity and example of always moving forward even when things got tough? When we were thrown into the uncharted waters of disability, we didn't know what to do. But we watched, listened and learned, and ultimately, found joy! You are the reason Represent! exists. May your stories live on forever and may we continue to share the legacies you are creating.

## ROSALIE MASTALER

Rosalie loves to tell stories that open windows and doors for younger readers to see beyond the world that surrounds them. She also finds joy when they see themselves in books and are able to say, "Hey! They are just like me!". She advocates for disability visibility by creating entertaining children's literature and ultimately hopes to help kids understand the meaning of inclusion and friendship.

Rosalie was born and raised in Southern California, but currently lives near Austin, TX with her awesome husband and three rambunctious boys.

For more works from Rosalie check out *Hunter's Tall Tales* and don't forget to visit her website where you can find The Ultimate Book List—one of the largest databases of books that feature characters or real people with disabilities.
**@mastalerbookclub**
**www.RosalieMastaler.com**

## HUNTER MASTALER

Hunter is thirteen years old and loves everything about art, enjoys reading Japanese manga, is a competitive swimmer, and can play a mean game of ping-pong. He is the oldest of three boys and tends to be the ringleader of their abundant energy. If he could travel anywhere it would most likely be to Japan or the coast. He really likes to see new places and try different things. He is a young but active advocate, spreading education and humor with his social media presence, at speaking engagements, as an ambassador for the Jordan Thomas Foundation and a mentor to younger amputees.
**@Mastalerpartyof5**

## BRANT DAY | WATTLE & DAUB

Owner and operator of Wattle & Daub, a creative studio with aspirations of world domination and Jackie Chan Kung Fu marathons. Brant has been designing and illustrating for over ten years, always creating something silly, fun, or colorful. His dream is to make silly things full-time in an attempt to take over the world...or at least make a few people smile.

Brant was born in Saginaw, Michigan, raised in Suwanee, Georgia, but currently lives outside Austin, TX with his wonderful wife and four adorable monsters.

Follow Wattle & Daub on Instagram (@wattlendaub) to stay up to date with all of the fun things going on and drop a line with your best t-shirt idea!
**www.wattlendaub.com**

"A well-researched anthology of diverse biographies which celebrates persons with disabilities. These powerful stories of strength, persistence and resilience will inspire everyone to follow their dreams."

Maryann Cocca-Leffler, Disability Rights Advocate/ Author/ Illustrator
*Fighting for YES! The Story of Disability Rights Activist Judith Heumann*
*We Want to Go To School! The Fight for Disability Rights*

". . .bios of fascinating people pushing against society's limiting definitions of disability as they follow their dreams."

Annette Bay Pimentel, author of *All the Way to the Top*

"One of the challenges of writing biographical material is to take a wild tangle of events, emotions, and relationships and craft a narrative that defines the subjects. Hunter and Rosalie simplify the high moments in the lives of their subjects, crafting narratives that celebrate their successes."

Michael Frizell, bestselling author of *Bender* and the *Female Force* series

". . .a refreshing breath of air that shows the determined, indomitable spirit of those in the disability community. Expectations are shattered and limitations fade as children discover stories of those athletes, artists, and activists who refused to let their diagnosis dissuade them from achieving greatness."

Mary Mecham, Advocates for Disability Inclusion in Literature, President

"Mastaler introduces disabilities to children in a way that breaks down barriers. *Represent! Vol. 1* helps kids see the people in the story and the lessons learned by them can be helpful to everyone."

Jack Wallace, US Sled Hockey, Paralympian

"With diversity and inclusion gaining much needed momentum and awareness in our society, *Represent! Volume 1* is just what is needed in the world of kid lit! This dynamic book showcases the rich depth of diversity within the disabled community. Oftentimes disability is left out of conversations of diversity, equity, and inclusion, and Represent! pushes it to the forefront. Hunter and Rosalie do a fantastic job of writing a book for all audiences—both non-disabled and disabled. A must read!"

Patty Cisneros Prevo, Paralympic Gold Medalist and author of *Tenacious: Fifteen Adventures Alongside Disabled Athletes*

". . .an empowering anthology that fervently displays the incredible impact disability can play in one's life, and not in the way one might expect. Word after word, story after story, you feel inspired. Reading this book, you quickly realize that there is so much more to gain from a disability than could ever be lost."

Ryan Rae Harbuck, author of *When I Grow Up I Want to be A Chair*

Text copyright © 2024 by Rosalie and Hunter Mastaler | Illustrations © 2024 by Brant Day
All Rights Reserved. Printed in the United States of America
Published by Motina Books, LLC, Van Alstyne, Texas www.MotinaBooks.com
Library of Congress Cataloguing-in-Publication Data:
Names: Mastaler, Rosalie & Hunter | Day, Brant
Title: Represent! Vol. 1
Description: First Edition. | Van Alstyne: Motina Books, 2024
LCCN: 2023939844
Paperback - ISBN 979-8-88784-022-2  | Hardcover - ISBN 979-8-88784-023-9